MW01260120

Building Essential Writing Skills

GRADE 1

New York • Toronto • London • Auckland • Sydney
Mexico City • New Delhi • Hong Kong • Buenos Aires

Writers: Shira Evans, Immacula Rhodes
Editors: Maria L. Chang, Shira Evans
Cover design: Tannaz Fassihi; Cover art: Eefje Kuijl
Interior design: Shekhar Kapur; Interior art: QBS Learning
Produced with QBS Learning

ISBN: 978-0-545-85039-1
Copyright © 2017 by Scholastic Inc.
All rights reserved.
Printed in the U.S.A.
First printing, January 2017.

1 2 3 4 5 6 7 8 9 10   40   23 22 21 20 19 18 17

Table of Contents

Table of Contents

Lesson 4: Writing a Draft continued

Introduction

Help children master key writing skills with these standards-based activities, designed to help them become successful writers. The fun, engaging reproducible pages are grouped into lesson packets that provide targeted practice in writing sentences, producing different types of writing, exploring the structure of writing, writing a draft, reviewing and improving writing, and revising and editing. Use the lesson to introduce the skills in each packet, then have children complete the pages to reinforce the lesson. As they work through the packets, children learn and practice important skills and concepts, such as types of sentences, capitalization and punctuation, distinguishing fact from opinion, sequencing, adding details, word choice, and much more.

These versatile, ready-to-use practice pages can be used in many other ways:

- Select an activity page for use as a "do now" activity to help get children settled first thing in the morning. Simply stack copies of the page on a table for children to pick up as they enter the room. Then allow a specific amount of time, such as five minutes, for them to complete the activity.

- Preview the day's lesson with a related skills page. You can use the activity to find out what children already know about the topic.

- Alternatively, you can use an activity page to review a previously learned lesson, assess what children have learned, and determine where they need further instruction.

- Assign a skills page for children to complete independently, with a partner, in small groups, or for homework.

An answer key is provided at the back of the book so you can review answers with children. In doing so, you provide opportunities to discuss, reinforce, or extend skills to other lessons. Children can also share their responses and strategies in small groups. This collaboration will enable them to deepen their understanding or clarify any misunderstandings they may have about the skill or writing process.

Meeting the Standards

The activities in this book meet the following standards for Grade 1.

Writing

Children will:

- Write opinion pieces in which they introduce the topic or name the book they are writing about, state an opinion, supply a reason for the opinion, and provide some sense of closure.

- Write informative/explanatory texts in which they name a topic, supply some facts about the topic, and provide some sense of closure.

- Write narratives in which they recount two or more appropriately sequenced events, include some details regarding what happened, use temporal words to signal event order, and provide some sense of closure.

- With guidance and support from adults, focus on a topic, respond to questions and suggestions from peers, and add details to strengthen writing as needed.

- Participate in shared research and writing projects.

- With guidance and support from adults, recall information from experiences or gather information from provided sources to answer a question.

Language

Children will:

- Print all upper- and lowercase letters.

- Use common, proper, and possessive nouns.

- Use singular and plural nouns with matching verbs in basic sentences.

- Use personal, possessive, and indefinite pronouns.

- Use verbs to convey a sense of past, present, and future.

- Use frequently occurring adjectives.

- Use frequently occurring conjunctions (e.g., *and, but, or, so, because*).

- Use frequently occurring prepositions (e.g., *during, beyond, toward*).

- Produce and expand complete simple and compound declarative, interrogative, imperative, and exclamatory sentences in response to prompts.

- Use end punctuation for sentences.

- Use conventional spelling for words with common spelling patterns and for frequently occurring irregular words.

Lesson 1: What Is a Sentence?

Objective

Children will review basic sentence structure and types of sentences.
They will practice writing sentences.

Standards

- Produce and expand complete simple declarative, interrogative, imperative, and exclamatory sentences in response to prompts.

- Use end punctuation for sentences.

What You Need

Copies of this packet for each student; whiteboard and markers

What to Do

1. Write the following sentences on the board:

   The rabbit hops home.
   Do rabbits dig holes?
   Come here, rabbit!
   The rabbit moves fast!

   Tell children that they are sentence detectives—they will be investigating sentences in this lesson. Explain that all sentences start with a capital letter. They end with a punctuation mark. Invite two volunteers to come to the board. One should circle the capital letters. Using a second color, the other should circle the punctuation marks. Distribute copies of "Is This a Sentence?" (page 8) and have children complete the top section.

2. Use the sentences above to review the four different types of sentences. Distribute copies of "State It," "Ask It," "Command It!" and "Exclaim It!" (pages 9–12). Have children practice writing different kinds of sentences.

3. Tell children that sentences have a subject. The **subject** is what the sentence is about. Review the sentences on the board. Have a volunteer draw a box around the subject in each sentence (rabbit). The "telling part" (**predicate**) tells what happens. Invite another volunteer to underline the telling part of each sentence. Distribute copies of "All About Bears" (page 13). Have children draw a box around the subject in each sentence and underline the telling part.

4. Use "Panda Punctuation" (page 14) to review punctuation.

> ★ A **sentence** tells a complete thought. It begins with a capital letter. It ends with a punctuation mark.

Is This a Sentence?

Read. Check ✓ the sentence.

1. The bear sits ☐

   The bear sits. ☐

2. My cat likes milk. ☐

   my cat likes milk. ☐

3. The rabbit ☐

   The rabbit hops. ☐

4. A tiger runs fast. ☐

   a tiger runs fast. ☐

5. My dog. ☐

   My dog licks my face. ☐

6. A lion roars. ☐

   A lion roars ☐

Think of an animal. Write your own sentence.

_____

_____

_____

Building Essential Writing Skills: Grade 1 © Scholastic Inc.

Name: _____   Date: _____

> A telling sentence is called a **statement**. It ends with a period (.).

State It

Read the statement.

A rabbit hops home.

Write a statement about an animal. Use a period (.) at the end.

_____

- -

_____

_____

- -

_____

Now draw your animal.

Name: _____   Date: _____

 An asking sentence is a **question**.
It ends with a question mark (?).

Ask It

Read the question.

Do rabbits dig holes?

Write a question about an animal.
Use a question mark (?) at the end.

_____

- -

_____

- -

_____

Now draw your animal.

Building Essential Writing Skills: Grade 1 © Scholastic Inc.

> ⭐ Some sentences give a **command**. A command sentence
> ends with a period (.) or an exclamation point (!).

Command It!

Read the command.

Come here, rabbit!

Write a command for an animal.
Use an exclamation point (!) at the end.

_____

- -

_____

- -

_____

Now draw your animal.

Name: _____ Date: _____

An **exclamation** shows excitement, surprise, happiness, or anger. It ends with an exclamation point (!).

Exclaim It!

Read the exclamation.

That rabbit moves fast!

Write an exclamation about an animal.
Use an exclamation point (!) at the end.

_____

\- \-

_____

\- \-

_____

Now draw your animal.

Name: _____ Date: _____

 The **subject** is what the sentence is about. The **telling part** (or the **predicate**) tells what happens.

All About Bears

Read the sentences. Draw a box around the subject.
Underline the telling part.

Example: The bear sits on the ground.

1. Bears eat leaves and berries.

2. Bears sleep during the winter.

3. Baby bears are called cubs.

4. They run and play.

5. Mama bears protect the babies.

Write a sentence about bears. Include a subject and a telling part.

Building Essential Writing Skills: Grade 1 © Scholastic Inc.

Name: _____ Date: _____

Panda Punctuation

Read each sentence. Circle the correct
punctuation mark. Write it in the box.

1. My favorite animals are pandas ☐   **.**   **?**   **!**

2. Why are pandas so popular ☐   **.**   **?**   **!**

3. Pandas are really cute ☐   **.**   **?**   **!**

4. Pandas eat bamboo ☐   **.**   **?**   **!**

5. They eat 40 pounds a day ☐   **.**   **?**   **!**

6. Do you like pandas ☐   **.**   **?**   **!**

Pick one of the questions. Write an answer.

_____

_____

_____

_____

Building Essential Writing Skills: Grade 1 © Scholastic Inc.

Lesson 2: Purpose for Writing

Objective

Children will identify different kinds of writing and set a purpose for writing.

Standards

With guidance and support from adults, write opinion, informative, and narrative (story) pieces.

What You Need

Copies of this packet for each student; whiteboard and markers

What to Do

1. Draw or project a three-column chart on the board. Write these headings: *Opinion, Informative, Story.* Explain that the purpose of **opinion writing** is to share what we think. It is important to provide reasons. The purpose of **information** (or informative) **writing** is to share facts. We can find facts in books or on trusted websites. The purpose of **story writing** is to tell what happened. A story can be real or made up. We tell stories in the order they happen.

2. Have children call out examples of each type of writing that may be found in your classroom. Record them on the chart. If children are having trouble identifying opinion writing, provide some examples.

3. Distribute copies of "Why We Write" (page 16). This page can be used as a cover page for a notebook of student writing or a collection of writing samples for each type of writing.

4. Each type of writing in this section can be its own mini-lesson. It is useful to share mentor texts for each kind of writing. Use the activity pages in this section to help reinforce your classroom lessons.

There are many different purposes for writing. Writers may share an opinion, give facts, or tell a story.

Why We Write

Read about why we write. Then do the activity.

We write to tell our **opinion**. Opinion means what we think.

We write to tell **information**. Information means facts.

We write to tell **stories**. Stories can be real or made up.

They tell what happened.

Read each title. Match it to the correct type of writing.

1. | All About Cats | Opinion Writing

2. | Why I Love Cats | Story Writing

3. | Cat's First Day of School | Information Writing

Building Essential Writing Skills: Grade 1 © Scholastic Inc.

Name: _____ Date: _____

Terrific Turtles

Read what Cami wrote about turtles.
Then answer the questions.

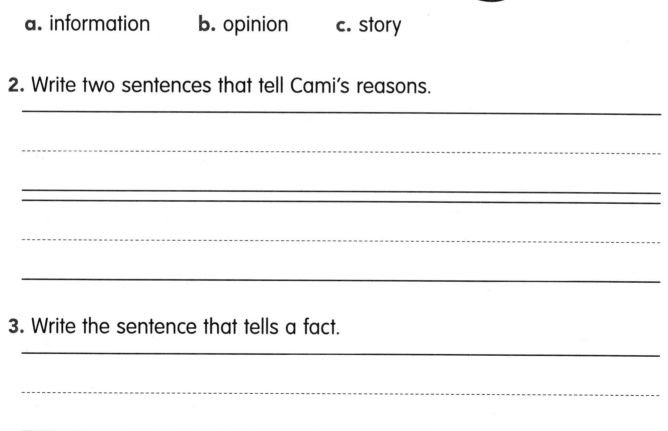

I think turtles are cool.

They have four legs and a shell.

Turtles are interesting.

They make fun pets.

1. What type of writing is this?

    a. information   **b.** opinion   **c.** story

2. Write two sentences that tell Cami's reasons.

_____

_____

_____

3. Write the sentence that tells a fact.

_____

_____

Name: _____ Date: _____

An **opinion** states what someone thinks or feels. A **fact** is a true statement.

Opinion or Fact?

Read each sentence. Circle *Opinion* or *Fact*.

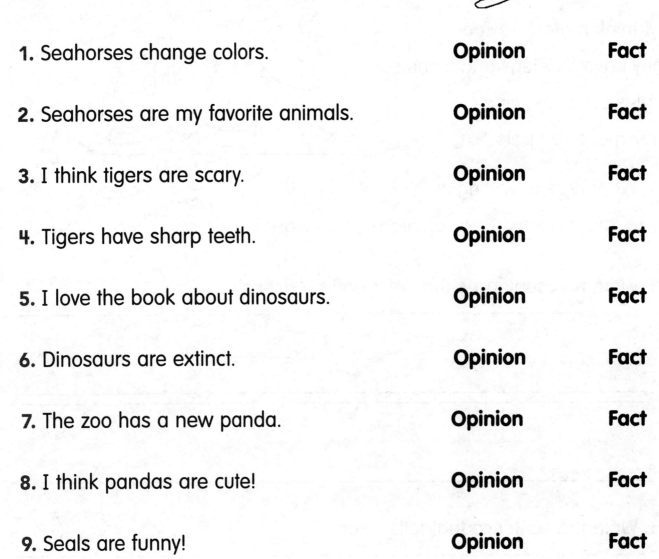

1. Seahorses change colors.	**Opinion**	**Fact**
2. Seahorses are my favorite animals.	**Opinion**	**Fact**
3. I think tigers are scary.	**Opinion**	**Fact**
4. Tigers have sharp teeth.	**Opinion**	**Fact**
5. I love the book about dinosaurs.	**Opinion**	**Fact**
6. Dinosaurs are extinct.	**Opinion**	**Fact**
7. The zoo has a new panda.	**Opinion**	**Fact**
8. I think pandas are cute!	**Opinion**	**Fact**
9. Seals are funny!	**Opinion**	**Fact**
10. Seals eat fish.	**Opinion**	**Fact**

Name: _____ Date: _____

 Telling information and giving facts are the main reasons for writing information pieces.

Just the Facts

Read the passage. Underline all the facts.

Miami, Florida
Thursday, October 5

A large snake was caught at Roland Park yesterday. It had escaped on Tuesday. The snake was 15 feet long. Many people in Florida own large snakes. The owner, Mike Jones, got his snake back.

1. What kind of writing is this?

   a. information   **b.** opinion   **c.** story

2. How do you know?

_____

_____

_____

Make sure all your details support the topic of your information piece.

Details, Details

Look at each word web. Cross out the detail that does not belong. Write why it doesn't belong.

1.

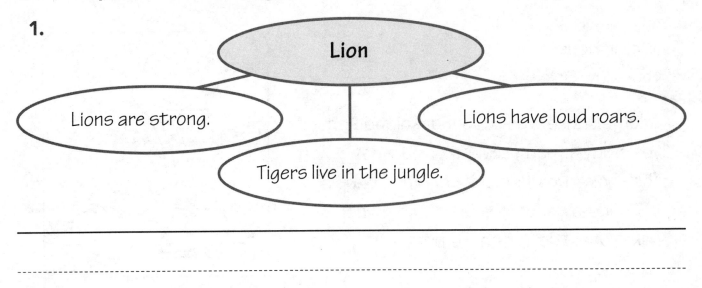

Lion

Lions are strong.

Lions have loud roars.

Tigers live in the jungle.

_____
- -
_____

2.

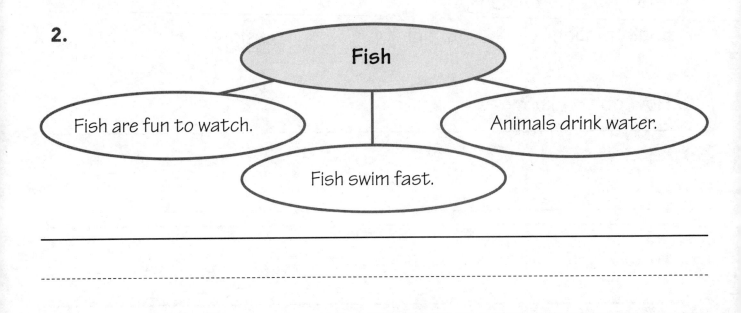

Fish

Fish are fun to watch.

Animals drink water.

Fish swim fast.

_____
- -
_____

Do research to find facts that you can use in your information writing.

Gather Your Facts

Choose an animal. Write it in the center of the web. Write three facts about the animal in the web. Look in books to help you.

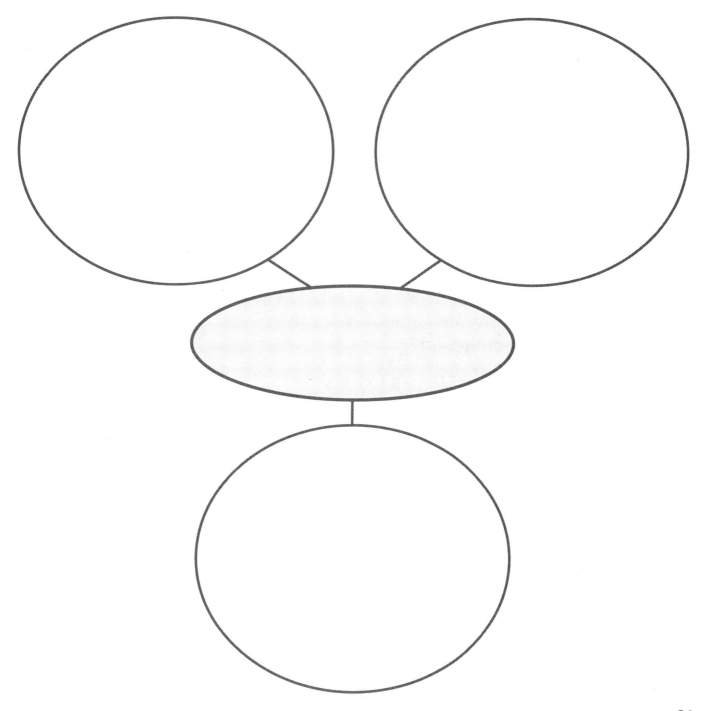

Name: _____   Date: _____

 A **story** tells about what happened.
It includes characters, setting, and a plot.

Horse Party

Read the passage.
Then answer the questions.

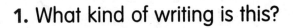

Harry the horse had a birthday.
He called all of his friends. They met in the big field.
Then they ate hay and carrots. Finally, they sang the
horse birthday song. It goes, "Nay, Nay, Nay, Hooray!"
Harry had the best birthday party ever.

1. What kind of writing is this?

   a. information   **b.** opinion   **c.** story

2. Who is the main character?

   a. Harry   **b.** Harry's friends

3. What is the setting? (Hint: The **setting** is where the story takes place.)

   a. carrots   **b.** the big field   **c.** Harry

4. What is the plot? (Hint: The **plot** is what happens.)

   a. Harry has a birthday party.

   b. Harry calls his friends.

   c. Harry eats hay and carrots.

Name: _____   Date: _____

The Surprise Gift

Look at the pictures. What happens first?

_____

_____
_____

_____

What happens next?

_____

_____
_____

_____

Name: _____ Date: _____

 Asking questions about a story can help you understand what's happening. *What* tells about the events. *Where* tells about a place. *Who* tells about the people.

Parts of a Story

Match each question word to the story part it tells about.

1. What?   characters

2. Where?   setting

3. Who?   plot

Read each sentence. Circle the question it answers.

4. My best friends are **Kelly** and **Ali**.   what?   where?   who?

5. We all went to **the park** today.   what?   where?   who?

6. We **rode bikes and played tag**.   what?   where?   who?

Use the sentences above to answer the questions.

7. What is the setting?

_____

8. Who are the characters?

_____

9. What is the plot?

_____

Lesson 3: Structure of Writing

Objective
Children will identify and write parts of a paragraph for different types of writing.

Standards
Write opinion, informative, and narrative pieces that include an introduction, supporting text appropriate for the type of writing, and a conclusion.

What You Need
Copies of this packet for each student; whiteboard and markers

What to Do

1. Write the following paragraph on the board:

   I like my house. There is a park nearby. I go there with my friends. We play soccer and basketball. We also ride bikes. I'm happy I live here.

2. Read the paragraph aloud to children. Explain that the first sentence tells what the paragraph is about. It tells the main idea. This is called the **introduction**. Invite a child to come to the board and underline the introduction.

3. Explain that the **conclusion** comes at the end of the paragraph. It can repeat the introduction in a different way. Ask another child to circle the conclusion.

4. Point out that the sentences between the introduction and conclusion are the **body** of the paragraph. These sentences give more information. In opinion writing, the body gives reasons for the opinion. In informative writing, it provides facts and details. The body tells about events in a logical order in story writing. Draw a box around the entire body of your paragraph. Then invite one volunteer at a time to read a sentence from the body.

5. Use the activity pages in this section to help reinforce your classroom lesson.

An **introduction** comes at the beginning of a paragraph. It tells what the paragraph is about.

Meow!

Jake is writing an opinion about cats. He has the body and conclusion. But he needs help with his introduction. Read what Jake wrote below. Then write an introduction for him.

Introduction:

_____

- -

_____

Body:

Cats are nice and quiet. My cat sits on my lap. I read to her.

Conclusion:

We are both happy!

Now read your introduction to a partner. Explain how it tells about the paragraph.

Name: _____ Date: _____

A **conclusion** comes at the end of a paragraph. It can repeat the introduction in a different way.

At the Zoo

Read what Eva wrote about the panda. Circle her conclusion.

The panda is the cutest animal at the zoo. It has black and white fur. Its eyes look so big and friendly! I always love to see the panda.

Now read Eva's opinion about monkeys. Write a conclusion for her.

The monkeys at the zoo make me laugh! I like to watch them swing from the trees. They hang by their tails while they eat.

_____

_____

_____

_____

_____

_____

★ The **body** of a paragraph comes between the introduction and conclusion. It gives information or details about the topic.

My 6th Birthday

Read Sal's story about his birthday.

My 6th birthday was great! I went to the movies with my dad. Then I came home. My mom opened the door. All my friends were waiting for me. We had pizza and cake. I felt so happy!

1. **Underline the introduction.**

2. **Circle the conclusion.**

3. **Write three things that the body tells you.**

_____

_____

_____

_____

_____

Name: _____   Date: _____

Time for School

Tom wrote about how he gets to school.
Then he mixed up the sentences.
Use numbers 1 to 4 to put the sentences
in order. Circle the sequence words.

_____ Then we wait together.

_____ I ride a bus to school every day.

_____ Finally, my bus comes and takes me to school!

_____ First, my mom walks me to the corner.

**Read about how Jack gets to school. Fill in the sequence words.
Use the words in the box.**

Finally	First	Then

Jack doesn't take a bus to school. He rides his bike!

_____, he puts on his helmet.

_____ he pedals to school.

_____, he locks up his bike.

A story follows an order from first to last. It ends with a conclusion.

Morning Surprise

**Put the pictures in order. Number the boxes from 1 to 4.
Then write a conclusion.**

_____

_____

_____

Lesson 4: Writing a Draft

Objective

Children will gather and organize information for different types of writing, and use their notes to write a draft.

Standards

- Focus on a topic to research and gather information about.

- Produce clear and coherent writing in which the development, organization, and style are appropriate to the purpose for writing (opinion, information, or storytelling).

What You Need

Copies of this packet for each student; whiteboard and markers

What to Do

1. Draw or display the organizer from "My Community" (page 32) on the board. Distribute copies of the page to children. Explain that an organizer helps them order their ideas. On the board, point out the topic sentence in the center. Read the sentence starter and fill it in. Have children do the same on their page. Then read the label on each detail circle. Demonstrate how to fill in each one. Ask children to record their ideas on their own organizer.

2. Tell children that the topic sentence will come at the beginning of their writing. This will be their introduction. Then have children decide the order in which they will write about the details. Have them number the detail circles from 1 to 3.

3. Pass out copies of the writing page labeled "Draft: My Community" (page 33). Tell children they will use the notes from their organizer to write a draft. Have them use the topic sentence for their introduction. Children can then write a sentence for each detail, putting the sentences in the predetermined order. Ask them to wrap up with a concluding sentence. Remind children that the goal in writing a draft is to write their ideas in complete sentences and to put them in order. They can correct errors in spelling and grammar later.

4. Use the organizers, activities, and writing pages in this section to help children prepare for and write drafts for different types of writing. Set their drafts aside for children to revisit during Lessons 5 and 6.

Name: _____ Date: _____

 An **organizer** helps you brainstorm and write your thoughts and ideas.

My Community

Think about your community. Use the organizer to take notes.

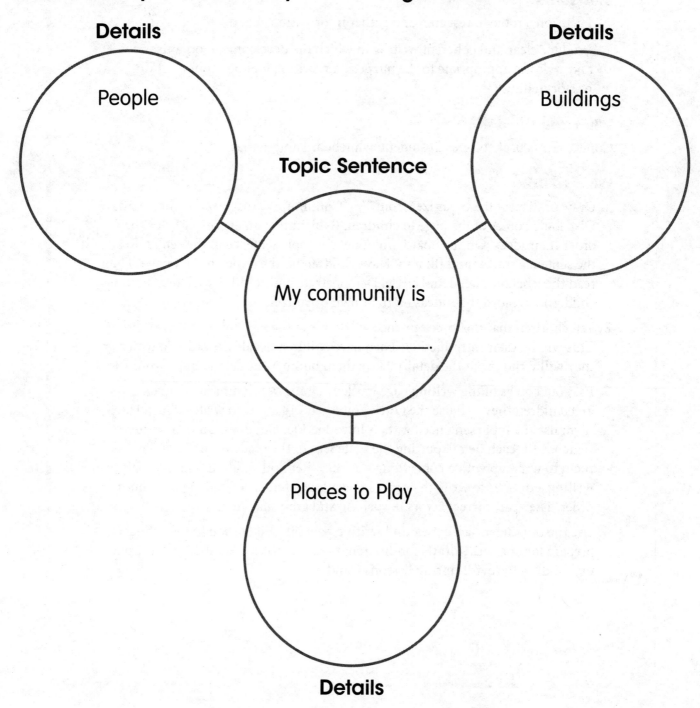

Details

People

Details

Buildings

Topic Sentence

My community is

_____.

Places to Play

Details

Draft: My Community

Write about your community. Use the ideas from your organizer.

My community is

_____

_____

_____

_____

_____

_____

_____

Name: _____ Date: _____

My Favorite Animal

Draw your favorite animal.
Write three reasons why you like this animal.

_____

- -

_____

_____

- -

_____

_____

- -

_____

Name: _____ Date: _____

Draft: My Favorite Animal

Write an opinion about your favorite animal.
Give reasons for why you like it.

_____

- -

_____
_____

- -

_____
_____

- -

_____
_____

- -

_____
_____

- -

_____
_____

- -

_____
_____

- -

_____

Name: _____ Date: _____

Diving Dolphins

Read the book review Matt wrote. Answer the questions.

I love the book *Dolphin's Playground*. It shows dolphins doing exciting things. The dolphins jump. They dive, too.

1. Write the sentence that shows Matt's opinion.

_____

- -

_____

2. Write the sentences that show Matt's reasons.

_____

- -

_____

- -

_____

Building Essential Writing Skills: Grade 1 © Scholastic Inc.

Name: _____ Date: _____ _____

Think about why you like a book.
Write your reasons on an organizer.

My Book Review

Choose a book to write about. Write the title in the chart. Fill in your opinion and reasons for it.

Title of book: _____

My opinion (what I think or feel about the book):

_____

_____

_____

_____

My reasons (why I like or don't like the book):

_____

_____

_____

_____

Draft: My Book Review

Write your book review. Tell your opinion and reasons for it.

_____

- -

_____

- -

_____

- -

_____

- -

_____

- -

_____

Check ✔ your work.

Words	Sentences	Punctuation and Grammar
☐ Spell words correctly.	☐ Use details.	☐ Start each sentence with a capital letter.
☐ Check for missing words.	☐ Use reasons to support opinion.	☐ Use the correct end punctuation.

Name: _____   Date: _____

Let's Play Soccer!

Read Alex's notes about how to play soccer.

1. two teams play the game

2. each team has a goal

3. players kick the ball down the field

4. they try to kick it into their team's goal

Now use his notes to write about how to play soccer. Write complete sentences. Use the back of this sheet if you need more space.

_____

- -

_____

_____

- -

_____

_____

- -

_____

Name: _____ Date: _____

How to Play

Work with a partner. Choose a sport or game that you both like.
Write notes about how to play it.

Name of sport or game: _____

_____

- -

1. _____
   _____

- -

_____

↓

_____

- -

2. _____
   _____

- -

↓

_____

- -

3. _____
   _____

- -

_____

Draft: How to Play

Write about your sport or game. Use your notes.

_____

- -

_____
_____

- -

_____
_____

- -

_____
_____

- -

_____
_____

- -

_____

Check ✓ your work.

Words	Sentences	Punctuation and Grammar
☐ Spell words correctly.	☐ Use details.	☐ Start each sentence with a capital letter.
☐ Check for missing words.	☐ Follow a logical order.	☐ Use the correct end punctuation.

When writing a story, put the events in the order they happen. Use sequence words like *first*, *next*, and *last*.

A Visit to the Library

Look at the pictures.
Which comes first? Write 1 in the box.
Which comes next? Write 2.
Which comes last? Write 3.

Now write a story. Tell about the events in order.
Use *first*, *next*, and *last*.

_____

_____

_____

_____

_____

_____

Name: _____ Date: _____

How to Get a Library Card

Read Margo's draft. Then rewrite the sentences. Put them in the correct order.

Getting a library card is easy!

Next, give it to the librarian.

Finally, check out a book.

Then, take your new card.

First, fill out a form.

_____

- -

_____

_____

- -

_____

_____

- -

_____

_____

- -

_____

_____

- -

_____

Name: _____ Date: _____

Double Dog!

**Read Jose's story. Put the sentences
in order. Number the boxes from 1 to 3.**

☐ My grandma adopted
a puppy for me, too!

☐ Now I have two dogs.

☐ My parents adopted a puppy
for me for my birthday. Guess what?

Now write about your pet. If you don't have a pet, make one up!

_____

_____

_____

_____

_____

Name: _____ Date: _____

 Remember to write about *who, what,* and *where* in your story. Tell the story in a logical order.

The Wrong Bag

Look at the pictures. They show twin brothers Ted and Ned. Write a story about what happened.

_____

- -

_____

- -

_____

- -

_____

- -

_____

Building Essential Writing Skills: Grade 1 © Scholastic Inc.

Name: _____   Date: _____

Perfect Pizza!

The pictures below show how to make a pizza.
Put the steps in order. Write 1 to 5 in the boxes.

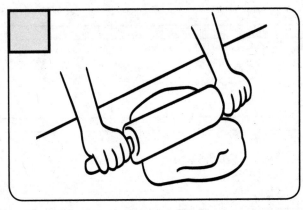

Building Essential Writing Skills: Grade 1 © Scholastic Inc.

Name: _____ Date: _____

How to Make a Pizza

Write out the steps to make a pizza.
Use the pictures on page 46 to help you.

Step 1:

_____

_____

Step 2:

_____

_____

Step 3:

_____

_____

Step 4:

_____

_____

Step 5:

_____

_____

Draft: How to Make a Pizza

Write about how to make a pizza. Use the steps from your organizer.

_____

- -

_____

- -

_____

- -

_____

- -

_____

- -

_____

- -

_____

- -

_____

Check ✓ your work.

Words	Sentences	Punctuation and Grammar
☐ Spell words correctly.	☐ Use sequence words.	☐ Start each sentence with a capital letter.
☐ Check for missing words.	☐ Follow a logical order.	☐ Use the correct end punctuation.

Building Essential Writing Skills: Grade 1 © Scholastic Inc.

Lesson 5: Pump Up Your Writing

Objective

Children will make their writing clearer and more interesting by using a variety of words and sentences.

Standards

Demonstrate command of the conventions of standard English grammar and its usage when writing.

What You Need

Copies of this packet for each student; whiteboard and markers

What to Do

1. Write the words *book* and *books* on the board. Read the words aloud. Tell children that both words are **nouns**. Then point to *book*. Explain that this word is a **singular noun**—it stands for only one book. The word *books* is a **plural noun**. It stands for more than one book. Use each word in a sentence.

2. Ask children to look at both words and tell how they are different. Point out the *s* at the end of *books*. Tell children that many singular nouns, like *book*, can be changed to a plural noun (*books*) by adding an *s* to the end of the word. Write a few more singular/plural word pairs on the board, such as *hat/hats*, *car/cars*, and *frog/frogs*. Review the words and their meanings with children.

3. Distribute copies of "My Busy Birthday" (page 50). Tell children they will decide if a singular or a plural noun should be used in each sentence. Complete the first sentence together. Then have children complete the rest of the page independently or with a partner. When finished, review and discuss their responses. If they chose an incorrect word, help them understand why it is not the best word choice for that sentence.

4. Conduct a similar mini-lesson for the other activity pages in this packet. Use the activities to provide practice and reinforcement in making word choices.

5. Have children take out and review their drafts from previous lessons. Ask them to reread their writing with a focus on word choice and grammar. Invite them to make corrections and changes to improve their writing.

A **singular** noun stands for one thing.
A **plural** noun stands for more than one.
You can add *s* to many nouns to make them plural.

My Busy Birthday

Read each sentence. Circle the best noun.

1. My birthday is going to be a busy _____.   day   days

2. My mom and I will shop for _____.   balloon   balloons

3. We will also buy a _____.   cake   cakes

4. Later, we will pick up my two best _____.   friend   friends

5. We will eat and play _____.   game   games

6. Everyone will sing the birthday _____.   song   songs

7. I can't wait to open all my _____!   present   presents

Name: _____ Date: _____

Who Does It Belong To?

Read each sentence. Fill in the blank with the correct pronoun.

my   **mine**

1. This is _____my_____ book.

2. This book is _____mine_____.

their   **theirs**

5. That is _____ ball.

6. That ball is _____.

our   **ours**

3. This is _____ kite.

4. This kite is _____.

your   **yours**

7. That is _____ bike.

8. That bike is _____.

Write about something you have. Use *my* and *mine*.

_____

_____

_____

_____

Name: _____   Date: _____

Pizza Time

Read each sentence. Choose the correct verb. Write it on the line.

1. I _____ to a great pizza place last week.   go   went

2. I _____ a pepperoni pizza.   has   had

3. I want to _____ there again today.   go   went

4. I _____ to get a vegetable pizza.   plan   planned

5. I _____ I will eat two slices.   think   thought

6. Last time I _____ four slices!   eat   ate

7. But I still _____ two slices home.   take   took

8. I hope to _____ you there!   see   saw

An **adjective** describes a noun.
It tells more about *what kind* or *how many*.

Describe It

Read each sentence.
Underline the adjective.

1. Here is your hot soup.

2. This pizza has three toppings.

3. We have a playful cat.

Describe the picture.
Use adjectives from the box.

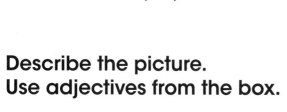

| green | happy | round | short | three |

_____

- -

_____

_____

- -

_____

_____

Name: _____ Date: _____

 Adjectives are describing words. Add adjectives to your writing to make it more interesting.

Cool Pool

Read Jack's draft. Circle the adjectives.

Yesterday was a hot day. I went to the public pool.

I stood on the bouncy diving board.

I dove into the cool water.

Write a sentence to finish Jack's story.
Use an adjective in your sentence.

_____

- -

_____

Name: _____   Date: _____

> ⭐ **Conjunctions** are used to connect words and ideas. Some conjunctions you can use in your writing are *and, but, so,* and *because.*

Late to the Library

Read each sentence.
Write the missing conjunction.
Use the words from the box.

and	but	so	because

1. I needed a book _____ I was writing about snakes.

2. My mom _____ sister went with me to the library.

3. We got there at 6:00 p.m. _____ it was closed.

4. We were hungry _____ we went to the diner instead.

Write a sentence about a time you were late.
Use a conjunction in your sentence.

_____

- -

_____

_____

- -

_____

Name: _____   Date: _____

 A **preposition** gives information about location, time, or movement. The prepositions *in* and *under* tell where (location), *during* and *after* tell when (time), and *around* and *toward* tell about movement.

My Book Bag

Read each sentence. Circle the correct preposition.

1. This morning I was walking _____ school.   to   during

2. I saw my friend come _____ me.   beyond   toward

3. He had my book bag _____ his hand.   in   from

Write an ending for the story. Use a preposition.

I was surprised! Then I remembered . . .

_____

- -

_____

- -

_____

- -

_____

Name: _____ Date: _____

> ⭐ The conjunction *and* can be used to join two words.
> For example, milk *and* cookies.

Around Town

**Read each sentence. Then expand the sentence.
Use *and* plus the word in parentheses.**

1. The movie theater sells candy. *(popcorn)*

The movie theater sells candy **and popcorn** .

2. There are houses on my street. *(trees)*

There are houses _____ on my street.

3. I went to the library yesterday. *(park)*

I went to the library _____ yesterday.

4. Buy eggs at the store, please. *(milk)*

Buy eggs _____ at the store, please.

Name: _____   Date: _____

The conjunctions *and* and *but* connect two things or ideas. *And* means the things or ideas are similar. *But* means they are different.

Near My House

Read each expanded sentence. Write *and* or *but* to complete the sentence.

1. There is a school _____ a library near my house.

2. There is a park _____ not a pool near my house.

Write your own expanded sentence. Use *and* or *but*.

_____

- -

_____

Lesson 6: Revising and Editing

Objective

Children will make corrections and revisions to improve their writing, and then produce a final copy.

Standards

- Focus on a topic, respond to questions and suggestions, and add details to strengthen writing.

- Produce different types of writing.

What You Need

Copies of this packet for each student; whiteboard and markers

What to Do

1. Write the following sentences on the board:

> *I lik bats.*
> *This my pen.*
> *dogs love to play!*
> *She has a new hat*

2. Tell children that each sentence on the board has a mistake. Read one sentence at a time. Ask children to help you find the mistake. Then discuss what needs to be done to correct the sentence.

3. Pass out copies of "Sensational Seahorses" (page 60). Explain that children will be finding and correcting mistakes in the draft on that page. If needed, help them get started by pointing out the first mistake and providing guidance to make the correction. Have children complete the page independently or with a partner.

4. Use the other pages in the packet to give children practice in correcting writing, adding details, and rewriting. Distribute copies of the template on page 63 for children to use for their rewriting.

5. Have children take out their drafts from previous lessons. Invite them to rewrite their text. Have them include revisions and corrections to produce a clean, final copy.

Name: _____   Date: _____

Sensational Seahorses

Read Charlie's draft. Circle the mistakes.

Seahorses cool. they use their tails to hold on. They change colors to hide? Seahorses are interesting animals

Rewrite Charlie's draft. Correct the mistakes.

_____

_____

_____

_____

_____

_____

_____

_____

_____

_____

_____

_____

⭐ All your sentences should support the main idea in a paragraph.

Horsing Around

Read Jon's draft about his favorite animal.

   Horses are my favorite animal. I love to see them run. Horses are beautiful. Cows live in fields. I hope to ride horses when I grow up!

Cross out the sentence that doesn't belong. Then write a sentence that does belong.

_____

_____

Now write another detail to add.

_____

_____

_____

Rewrite Jon's draft on another piece of paper. Make corrections and add details.

Name: _____   Date: _____

Doggie Details

Read Maggie's draft. Help her add more details.

You need to take good care of a dog.
First, you need to give it food and water.
Finally, you need to give it lots of love!

Which detail can Maggie add? Circle it.

a. You need to adopt a dog.

b. You need to walk it every day.

c. You need to sleep well.

Write one more detail for Maggie to add to her draft.

_____

- -

_____

_____

- -

_____

Rewrite Maggie's draft on another piece of paper.
Make corrections and add details.

Name: _____ Date: _____

Title: _____

_____

- -

_____
_____

- -

_____
_____

- -

_____
_____

- -

_____
_____

- -

_____
_____

- -

_____
_____

- -

_____
_____

- -

_____

Answer Key

p. 8
1. The bear sits.
2. My cat likes milk.
3. The rabbit hops.
4. A tiger runs fast.
5. My dog licks my face.
6. A lion roars.

pp. 9, 10, 11, and 12
Sentences and drawings will vary.

p. 13
1. Bears eat leaves and berries.
2. Bears sleep during the winter.
3. Baby bears are called cubs.
4. They run and play.
5. Mama bears protect the babies.
Sentences will vary.

p. 14
1. . 2. ? 3. . or ! 4. .
5. . or ! 6. ?
Answers will vary.

p. 16
1. Information Writing
2. Opinion Writing
3. Story Writing

p. 17
1. b
2. Turtles are interesting.
   They make fun pets.
3. They have four legs and
   a shell.

p. 18
1. Fact 2. Opinion 3. Opinion
4. Fact 5. Opinion 6. Fact
7. Fact 8. Opinion 9. Opinion
10. Fact

p. 19
All the sentences in the paragraph
should be underlined.
1. a
2. Answers will vary.

p. 20
1. Tigers live in the jungle.
   This detail is not about lions.
2. Animals drink water.
   This detail is not about fish.

p. 22
1. c 2. a 3. b 4. a

p. 23
Answers will vary. Sample answer: The
girl gets a gift basket. Inside the basket
is a puppy.

p. 24
1. plot 2. setting 3. characters
4. who? 5. where? 6. what?
7. the park 8. Kelly and Ali
9. Sample answer: Friends were having
   fun in the park.

p. 26
Introductions will vary.

p. 27
Children should circle the last sentence
of the first paragraph. Conclusions for
the second paragraph will vary.

p. 28
1. Children should underline the first
   sentence.
2. Children should circle the last
   sentence.
3. Answers will vary.

p. 29
3, 1, 4, 2; circle *Then, Finally*, and *First*
First, Then, Finally

p. 30
3, 2
1, 4
Conclusions will vary.

p. 36
1. I love the book *Dolphin's Playground*.
2. It shows dolphins doing exciting
   things. The dolphins jump. They
   dive, too.

p. 39
Children should use a logical sequence
to write about how to play soccer.
Sample answer: It takes two teams to
play soccer. First, each team chooses
a goal. Then the players kick the ball
down the field. They try to kick it into
their own goal. If the ball goes in, the
team scores!

p. 42
3, 1, 2

p. 43
Getting a library card is easy!
First, fill out a form.
Then, take your new card.
Next, give it to the librarian.
Finally, check out a book.

p. 44
2, 3, 1

p. 46
5, 3, 2, 1, 4

p. 50
1. day 2. balloons 3. cake
4. friends 5. games 6. song
7. presents

p. 51
3. our 4. ours 5. their
6. theirs 7. your 8. yours

p. 52
1. went 2. had 3. go
4. plan 5. think 6. ate
7. took 8. see

p. 53
1. hot 2. three 3. playful

p. 54
Children should circle these words:
hot, public, bouncy, cool

p. 55
1. because 2. and 3. but 4. so

p. 56
1. to 2. toward 3. in

p. 57
1. The movie theater sells candy
   and popcorn.
2. There are houses and trees
   on my street.
3. I went to the library and park
   yesterday.
4. Buy eggs and milk at the
   store, please.

p. 58
1. and 2. but

p. 60
Seahorses are cool. They use their tails
to hold on. They change colors to hide!
Seahorses are interesting animals.

p. 61
Children should cross out this sentence:
Cows live in fields.
Answers will vary.

p. 62
b
Answers will vary.